You expect a new book of poems by Gordon Meade to be full of weather, birds, fish and animals (including humans). *Sounds of the Real World* doesn't disappoint. In his deceptively simply matter-of-fact, sharply observant way, Meade delineates our relationship with the natural world and with each other, adding a dollop of zen wisdom. And running through the book is Meade's passion, the sea, like life both 'wavering and constant'.

Hamish Whyte,
author of *The Unswung Axe*

To read Gordon Meade's poems is to feel you've met the man, walked and talked with him and shared his way of looking at the world with an acutely observant eye and a wry and imaginative mind. A poet who is a life companion.

Diana Hendry,
author of *Late Love & Other Whodunnits*

In theme and subject-matter these poems are a satisfying consolidation of and extension to Gordon Meade's previous work. The vicissitudes of tide and weather, the creatures that are his motifs – from the slugs ground under his father's heel to the ghostly gorillas at Heidelberg Zoo – and the vagaries of his own heredity … all are depicted with clarity and vitality, the familial poems instilling a sense of lurking unease. His smooth-flowing stanzas and compelling rhythms are permeated by a distinctive yet ever-varying quality of light, most penetrating when they conjure up glimmerings of ourselves. For though he rightly describes his as 'a watching brief', it is his vivid and perceptive interpretation of this that makes the volume the pleasurable assemblage of illuminations it is.

Stewart Conn,
author of *The Breakfast Room*

for Wilma and Sophie

Gordon Meade is a Scottish poet who now lives in London.

Over the past twenty years or so he has divided his time between his own writing, devising creative writing courses for vulnerable young people in a variety of different settings and reading from his own work in the United Kingdom, Belgium, Luxembourg and Germany.

He has also been a Fellow in Creative Writing at the Duncan of Jordanstone College of Art, Writer in Residence for Dundee District Libraries and a Royal Literary Fund Writing Fellow attached to the University of Dundee.

Sounds of the Real World is his seventh collection of poetry.

Sounds of the
Real World

Also by Gordon Meade

The Familiar Arrowhead Press (2011)
The Private Zoo Arrowhead Press (2008)
The Cleaner Fish Arrowhead Press (2006)
A Man at Sea diehard publishers (2003)
The Scrimshaw Sailor (1996 Chapman Publishing)
Singing Seals (1991 Chapman Publishing)

Sounds of the Real World

Gordon Meade

Cultured Llama Publishing

First published in 2013 by
Cultured Llama Publishing
11 London Road
Teynham, Sittingbourne
ME9 9QW
www.culturedllama.co.uk

ISBN 978-0-9926485-0-3

Printed in Great Britain by Lightning Source UK Ltd

Jacket design by Mark Holihan
Front cover image courtesy of Allan Shedlock
Copy editing by Anne-Marie Jordan

Contents

I am the family face;
Flesh perishes, I live on.

Thomas Hardy

Part One

Smithereens

Heredity

To my father, animals
were animals and humans,
humans. Slugs were slugs.
And worms were there
to be dug up and used
as bait to catch fish.

To my mother, humans
were not to be trusted
and animals were easier,
by far, to live with.
She believed she could talk
to them and that they listened
to her; they understood.

Like most of us, I have
a bit of both of them in me.
There are some humans
I feel I can count on and some
animals I think I can get through to.
I have never liked eating fish,
and worms and slugs are
best left well alone.

Slugs

Before the invention of pellets
my father had his own way of ridding
our vegetable patch of slugs.

He would sprinkle them with salt.
Sometimes, he would do it by himself
slinking off after Sunday lunch

with the salt cellar secreted
about his person. At other times,
he would take me with him

and would insist that I watch.
At first, the white crystals, like napalm
from above, would merely stop

the creatures dead in their glistening
tracks. Then, it would start to seep into them,
fizzing silently. Part of the process,

if I remember correctly, involved
a lot of lathering. By the end, the slugs
looked like tiny whales that had,

far out at sea, taken a wrong
turn and found themselves washed
up on a deserted beach. I was

not allowed to touch them.
My father's heel would grind the remains
into the earth. As on our fishing

trips, so with our ferocious
gardening; my father always did the killing.
Mine was just a watching brief.

Flounders and Eels

These are the sorts of things
that no-one really wants to find
on the end of their lines; these, and clumps
of weed, or the proverbial old boot.

Neither one is any good, especially
if it is trout that you are after. I had
to laugh at the amount of times, when my father
and I used to fish the River Earn,

that a flatfish or an exaggerated
worm would arise from the depths either
flapping or twirling. The flounders were easy
to get rid of; more often than not

the hooks would just slide free from
their gaping mouths. Eels were a different
kettle of fish. They usually swallowed the barb
and could give you a nasty cut with

their razor-sharp fins. In the end,
I often just cut the line and let them
drop back down into the river with a splash.
My father, on the other hand,

would nearly always reel them
in, then dash their heads against
a nearby rock, before opening them up
in order to retrieve his stolen lure.

The River Earn

To begin with, the River Earn was a river
of fish – a salmon river – but also a provider
of brown and rainbow trout, of black

eels and speckled flounders. It was also
a river of boredom. One on whose banks
I stood and watched my father, filled

to the brim with patience, cast fly after fly
into its stilled middle wherein, he believed,
the largest salmon lived. It was also

the first and last river I ever managed
to walk across. One particularly bitter winter
it froze over, and one morning I inched

my way to the other side. I can still
remember the sound of creaking hinges
and the hairline cracks that suddenly

appeared. At times, it felt as if I was
walking across a sheet of polished glass –
not the reinforced sort you can get

today – but one that, at any moment,
might well have given way; might just as
easily have shattered into smithereens.

A Leech

Only once, as a child
in a nearby pond, have I ever felt
one tugging at my skin.

Looking down, through
fresh water, I could see it, no more
than two inches of black

flesh, loosely attached to
my ankle. Very slowly, I lifted my foot
out of the water and watched

as it flopped inertly against
my white skin. All I had to do was gently
roll it off and let it plop back

down into its shallow depths.
This I did with a slight tinge of regret.
It had not grown at all

and never really had the chance
to savour my blood. As they say, there
had been no exchange of

bodily fluids. The idea of its life
as a parasite remained, both for me
and itself, a fiction. All it was

that day was yet another
creature, briefly observed, and then,
ever so casually, flicked away.

The Bat

It was my mother's screams that alerted us
to its existence. We, my father and I, were down-
stairs in the kitchen. I was halfway through

a bowl of cereal and he was lathered up
for shaving. Both of us dropped everything and ran
upstairs. My mother stood in the middle

of the bedroom, petrified and all screamed
out. All she could manage was a strangled, 'Get it
out of here!' The 'it' in question being a bat

flickering its way, at head height, in an erratic
circle, around the room. After a while, it landed on
one of the curtains and my father cupped it

in his hands. Before allowing it to escape, he let
me see it, stretching out a paper-thin wing between
his finger and thumb and inviting me to

stroke it with one of mine. The bat flew
through the bedroom window and away. Turning
back to the middle of the room, I watched

as my mother sat slumped on the bed, ashen-
faced and coated in sweat. 'Disgusting creature…
disgusting creature…' was all she said.

Bluebottles

Even to this day, I am unsure
as to whether that is the proper name
for them, or if they ever existed

at all. Bluebottles was what
my mother used to call them. To me,
they looked just like flies,

although maybe a bit bigger.
But to her, they were a different species
altogether. Flies were dirty

but bluebottles were disgusting;
carriers of every disease known to man.
And it didn't end with them.

Bluebottles were revolting,
but if you were ever unlucky enough
to see a cleg, usually atop

a cow-pat, you had better run
like hell. A single bite from one of them
and you were done for.

Divine Thoughts

I remember watching a cat
playing with mice in my father's
store-room; pouncing

on them, pinning them down,
trapping them by their tails, releasing
them, and catching them again.

All of this set against a back-
drop of sacks of grain, illuminated
by the odd shaft of sunlight.

Looking back on it, it was
my first memory of how I thought
a god might behave.

The Good Dog
for Walter Bacham

This morning I told our dog I loved her,
but she did not understand my words. Then,
I told her she was a good dog. At that, she raised
her head and wagged her tail. It all goes

to show how much she really understands.
She is not a human, nor is she a creature of
the wild. She does not feel that she is loved but
she does, however, know that she is good.

The Past

Rain is like a forest.
The further away it is
the harder it is
to see through it.

It is the same
with the past. In order
to try and understand it,
to come to terms

with it, you have to
find a way to bring it back,
to get it up close and personal,
to not just remember it,

but to feel it, to touch
it and smell it, to taste it
and hear it, to see it, right there
in front of your eyes, as if

you never really left it
behind. Poetry is a way
to do that, as are
alcohol and nightmares.

The Whisky Drinker

Does the first sip always promise
what the final swallow is sent to deliver?

To start with, the illusion of incisiveness but,
in the end, disaster. Oblivion is all he is really after.

He can lecture you for hours on the different shades
of peat, the subtle influences of seaweed and the smokiness
this particular malt inhaled inside the darkness of its barrel;

but the end result is always the same – himself
lying wrecked on his favourite sofa with his arm
wrapped around another empty bottle.

Stainless Steel

There is nothing romantic
about an attempted suicide.
There is nothing even sad

about it. It is all violence. It is
all aggression. Once, I found myself
sitting next to a friend who was

in the process of trying to slash
his wrists. He tried his best but couldn't
get the blade to go in deep

enough. In the end, defeated,
he handed it to me. We sat together
for a while, and then he watched

me leave. We were somehow
both exhausted by it; him by his
failed attempt, and me

from watching it. There was
nothing romantic about it. It was all
just stainless steel and blood.

There are no facts only interpretations.

Friedrich Nietzsche

Part Two

Man's Work

Park Life
for Wilma

It was not my idea of a night out
in East London, to find ourselves, approaching
midnight, trapped in a park. Luckily,

our only companions were a pair
of foxes which were as surprised to see us
there as we were ourselves –

the best laid plans, etc. We had
intended to cross the park to the local Tube
station as the gate was still open.

When we reached the other side,
the exit there was locked and, when we retraced
our footsteps back to where we had

entered, so was it. We tried to clamber
over the fence, but it was too high and we were
too old. We called the police, who rang

the council, who sent a man, on stand-
by to release us, which he did, very promptly
and with good grace. To save face,

I lied, explaining to him that I thought
the park was locked up at midnight. He also lied,
when he told me it was always shut

by eleven. It was only when we got
back home that we began to realise how lucky
we had been. We had not been

frightened by the foxes, but were so
now, retrospectively, by a chance encounter
with an imaginary gang of humans.

"the best laid plans" is a reference to, and a misquote from the Robert Burns'
poem 'To A Mouse'. The title of the poem was stolen from the Blur song of the
same name.

Supermarket Sweep

This time there are no questions to be
answered, at least not by the participants.
This time there are no time limits, no inflatable
bonuses and no camp presenter. This time

you are allowed to use any means you think
necessary to get what it is you want. And this time
the prize at the end of the show is your hooded face
on the telly and as much loot as you can carry
past the occasional burnt-out home.

Spare Ribs

There is always a woman behind it
all … He killed his children to get back
at his ex … He stabbed his wife

and his two daughters before killing
himself … A woman has been found in the shed
of the man who ran amok near the Christmas

market. As if they were the reason
for it. As if the victims were to blame. As if
all the violence done to womankind

by man was, in some way, revenge;
a sort of payback for the first spare rib
they stole from him in order to exist.

The Break of Day
After Paul Delveaux

It is almost impossible to tell whether
they are women in the process of becoming trees,
or trees abandoning their roots in order

to embrace a different kind of being.
And what about the single man in the distance?
What would he care to imagine as he

makes his way slowly towards the edge
of the composition? Would he rather have the women
planted firmly in the ground beside him,

or have the trees more mobile, so that
no matter where he found himself, they would
always be there for him to rely on?

An Open Grave

This morning, the body
of a dead rabbit that hitherto
had lain unmarked,

except by a family of crows,
was finally recognised – a small head-
stone, a cairn of seashells

and a handful of daffodils.
My first instinct was that it had been
the work of a child and then,

a girl. It must have been
a girl, maybe even a mother and her
daughter. It was somehow

not the sort of thing you would
have imagined a boy or a man doing,
not even a father and his son.

All things being equal,
they would probably have just
left it to the crows.

The Rook Shoot

The rooks, that had
before circled like smoke
above the tops

of the beech trees
and the oaks, are now falling
through their branches

like so many lumps
of coal. And this is man's
work, I am told.

Till Death Do Us Part

At thirteen, I pretended, at first,
only to myself, but then to all my friends,
that the girl I had dated on holiday,

and then been dumped by, had died
abruptly from a rare disease. It somehow made
it easier for me to imagine her

deceased rather than continuing
to live her life without me. It meant that I got
loads of sympathy instead of ridicule.

It became harder, the older I got,
to maintain the same sorts of fiction regarding
subsequent failed romances. Some

of my ghostly exes would, on occasion,
be spotted in the flesh by people I had
told of their demise. In the end, I had

to own up, but still I lied: it was me
who had ended it not them. They had all wanted
to remain friends. But I had no desire

to show them any kindness. Once it was
over, all I wanted was, if not an actual death, then
at the very least, an unmistakable end.

Old Thoughts

Poetry is like writing
down the thoughts you used
to have as a child
that you knew were just
too old for you.

Does anyone else
really get this? Does anyone
out there really
understand what it is that
I am trying to convey?

Like, I know it was
wrong for me to be happy
when my grandmother
died. But I also know that
that was what I felt

and for the right
reasons. She would no
longer be a burden
for my mother and father.
But there was just

no way I could
actually say that to any-
one. So, like so many
unexpressed thoughts, it
just went under-

ground for a while.
In its case, over fifty years.
But now, it has raised
its not so ugly head and
demanded to be said.

A Good Death

One of the best I have ever seen
was on the silver screen – Marlon Brando's
in *The Godfather, Part One*.

He, whose character had been
behind the violent deaths of so many others
in the film, was allowed to pass

away while playing with his grandson
in the garden. A lot of religions talk about the advantages
of having had a good death; one for which

you have prepared yourself; one which
will send you well on your way to the longed for afterlife.
And yet, it seems, there is no justice,

in either how you go, or when; both
the good and the bad having equal chances
of either dying young or hanging on.

Why I Want a Sky Burial

There was never a coffin worth a dime.
                                    – Jim Harrison

I like the idea that the undertaker, before
he can begin, feels the need of a stiff drink.

I do not think that has ever been the case
in any of the funerals I have attended. I also like
the fact that, after the ceremony, all my relations
will get a decent feed; flesh and bones, instead

of the usual fare, triangular sandwiches and tepid
tea. But what I like most is that, in the end, there will
be nothing left of me but bones; no ashes filling up
a plastic urn, no rotting flesh decomposing underground.

As I have lived my life, with appetites aplenty; so,
after the last prayer wheel has ceased to roll, every morsel
of my mortal self will have been swallowed whole.

Four Candles

Friends of ours have given us four square
candles, each with a single word written on one side
and the Chinese symbol for that word printed

above it – Peace, Energy, Wisdom and Love.
Each of the candles is individually wrapped in cellophane.
In order to light one, we would have to unwrap it,

tease out the wick, strike a match and watch it
burn. In a given number of hours, the candle would be
gone. There would either be no more wisdom left,

a distinct lack of energy, a cooling of our love
or, worst of all, a declaration of war. We have decided,
for the time being, to keep them under wraps.

Right and Wrong

How old or how young were we
when we first realised that right and wrong
are almost always relative terms?

Was it during a history lesson
when we saw that what was right for the settlers
was definitely wrong for the natives?

Or was it in a biology class
when we learnt that what worked for the parasite
was quite the opposite for the host?

Whenever it was that it started, it still remains
the same. That which gives pleasure to the winner
must always bring the loser pain.

Praise the sea, on shore remain.

John Florio

Part Three

Seasoned With Salt

Fishing

A great blue heron, as the tide
comes in, follows it in, ransacking each
pool in turn, just before their rims

are overwhelmed and they give
themselves up to the anonymity of the sea.
The fish in the pools are frantic;

knowing in their many bones that,
at any moment, they will be either dead
or free. It is this frisson the heron

loves the most. As he swallows down
the last fish's forlorn hopes he can almost
taste its fear, seasoned with salt.

Water and Stone

The breakwater stands for nothing,
this afternoon. It just lies down on what, for
the moment, is the bottom of the sea

and lets the top of it wash over it. Not
that the breakwater has ever really stood
for anything. They have only been

the imaginings of people like myself who,
dissatisfied with what the real world has to offer
them, have tried to make more of it. Today,

exhausted by the effort, I cannot see
past the hard facts of water, concrete and
stone. Today, the breakwater does

not stand at all and, I too, like it, have
decided to just lie down and let the sounds
of the breaking waves wash over me.

The Other Side

The other side looked
so bright, yesterday, so inviting,
bathed in brilliant sunshine.

I wonder if we looked the same
to it. Today started out grey and now,
at around noon, the other side

has disappeared. All I can see
are a few hundred yards of sea and then,
nothing. It is as if the other side

has ceased to exist, has, in fact,
never existed at all. In the minds of those
on the other side, our existence

must also have been
called into question. Maybe tomorrow,
the sun will shine again

and, once more, we will
all know where we stand in
relation to the other.

Hit by Spray

The sea likes to remind us,
sometimes, that it is still here;
that is has always been here;
that it will never leave us. The sea
has to do this, sometimes;

just in case we have forgotten
it; just in case we have begun to
take it for granted; just in case
we are no longer aware that we our-
selves are also made of water.

Terns

for Sophie

The sky is so bright, sometimes,
and the sea so white, that, as with skylarks,
we become aware of terns first

through their songs. Then we track
them down as they surf through the air on
the lookout for sand-eels. When

they see them they dive, though not
like gannets, straight down, but with a twirl
at the end that is all their own.

They rise differently as well, as if
they are reluctant to leave the sea behind
them. They take the silver back

home with them to feed their young,
but it is the taste of the salt water on their
tongues that they will miss the most.

The Sounds of the Real World

Sometimes I can hear
the sounds of the real world…

a delivery van comes to a halt,
leaves its engine running, drops the morning
papers at the side of the road,
and then, moves on…

a bus arrives, slows down
and stops, opens and closes its door,
with a whoosh, and then, is gone…

a special correspondent, somewhere
in the Middle East, sheltering from the latest crossfire,
delivers his world into the living room, and then,
at the flick of a switch, is done.

Sometimes I can hear
the sounds of the real world…

the shriek of a herring gull
as it realises its catch is about to be
stolen by another…

the stumbling to its knees
of an exhausted wave after it has crossed,
if not the Seven Seas then, at least,
the width of the Firth…

and the open-handed slap
of a creel as it begins its descent on nothing,
but the end of a rope, to the bottom
of the sea.

Sometimes, I can hear
the sounds of the real world.

Love Apples

Our desire for cheap, home-
grown fare has overridden our love
of the dramatic view.

Two tomato plants are vying
for the distinction of obliterating
the sea. Just a few weeks

in situ and they have already
greened-out the bottom row of panes.
I can still see the tops of the waves

and most of the sky. The rocky
shore and the breakers have disappeared,
as has the breakwater, my constant

companion during the past few
years. It is that length of rock and concrete
that I shall miss the most. I doubt

if the taste of our garden salads
will be able to compensate for the loss –
the salty water sliding over it,

the occasional cormorant drying
its wings on it, and the single heron perched
upon it, before deciding where to fish.

Angles of Attack

As the tide is turning, there
comes a time when both the angle
of the breakwater to the rocky shoreline,
and the angle of the harbour wall

to the shore road, have a strange
effect on the sea. It looks as if the tide is
both coming in and going out. Waves break on top
of each other. Some collide head-on

at right angles, while others just
drive on through. After the moment has
passed, things go back to normal. The waves come
in, regular as clockwork, and then,

uniformly, go out. Like most, I am
reassured by the sea's constancy, but what
I really look forward to is the moment when the disparate
angles start to kick in and all hell breaks loose.

A Sign

There is a dull grey shimmer
on the surface of the water in the harbour
and the same sort of restlessness

you get as it starts to simmer
in a pan. Although it is not hot, it looks
as though it should be. Above

the surface, there is a sign
I cannot make out and, beyond that,
the open sea. It, too, is grey

but unmistakably cold.
The movement is different too. Like
a carpet being unrolled, or

a blanket smoothed. My eye
keeps returning to the water enclosed
by the arms of the harbour.

I like that shimmer. I like
the idea of its imaginary simmer. And,
most of all, I like the fact

that I cannot read the words
that someone, sometime or other, made
the effort to nail above it.

A Sort of Homecoming

The sea is in
one of its strange moods,
forever threatening
to turn brown.

I would like to say
it is gun-metal grey but
it is more the colour
of a faded saddle-bag

like the ones I used
to see in Westerns. The tops
of the waves still manage
to keep their heads

above the water
from which they are
made. Pure white, the only
way they can escape

the general drabness
is by dashing themselves
against the rocks. Further out
there is no such luck.

They have to wait
until they have been
carried to the shore. Like so
many ships before

them, they will come
to realise that the biggest
danger lies when you are
closest to home.

Zen and not Zen

I am afraid
I just cannot see
more than what is
in front of me

and more
often than not
it is the sea.
I know the drill –

before you start
practising, mountains
and rivers are
mountains and rivers –

and when you are
practising, mountains
and rivers are no longer
mountains and rivers –

and after you stop
practising, mountains
and rivers are mountains
and rivers again

but not the same.
And a part of me
gets all that. But
before, during

and after practising,
for me the sea will
always remain
the sea – both real

and imaginary –
both coming
and going – both
breaking and calm.

A Love of the Sea

It is a sort of faith; a kind of belief
and, like so many, it is both wavering
and constant. In other words,

it comes and goes; it advances
and recedes. At times, I doubt it and,
at others, it is strengthened;

even when I turn my back on it.
I have many rituals concerning it
but none I care to mention.

Our relationship is both complicated
and straightforward. I love it, but I am
scared of it. I love living

beside it but not crossing over it.
I know that it will always be there in
the background even when I

cannot hear it. The sacrifice it would
ask of me I will never grant it. I would
rather do anything than drown.

Should the truth about the world exist,
it's bound to be non-human.

Joseph Brodsky

Part Four

A Fate Worse Than Death

The Deer

For me, the real hero of *The Deer Hunter*
is the deer itself; the one that gets away. The one
that never makes it to Vietnam; the one

that manages to avoid the draft by hiding
in the woods. The only danger it has to face is
in the scene it shares with Robert De Niro;

the one that goes against his character's
philosophy of Just One Shot. Just one shot; only this
time it is up into the air and a palpable miss.

In the film, we see everything that happens
to the human characters, but the deer just disappears over
the brow of a hill and is never mentioned again.

The Gorillas: Armistice Day at Heidelberg Zoo

Are they ghosts, these three?
To me, they seem to be. Or are they,
possibly, pensioners, they surely might be.
Or are they just us, stripped of both

our clothes and our dignity? Are they not
the forgotten whom we dare not remember?
Or are they, perhaps, the long-term prisoners
of our idle curiosity? Are they what we used

to be or, rather, what we still might yet
become? The lost and the lonely, confined
behind concrete, glass and steel; without the chance
of ever making contact with anything that's real.

Success

The dominant species in Africa is no
longer the lion but the hyena. That is to say
that hyenas kill more of their own prey than lions
do. It is more likely that a lion would be

seen scavenging the kill of a hyena than
the other way round. I find it all very strange.
I was always told, by anyone who was interested
in telling me, that lions were the best hunters

and hyenas just had to hang around until
the pride had had their fill before moving in
for the scraps. This latest bit of information has
flipped my whole world view head over heels.

It would be like saying that the most admired
artists of any genre you might care to mention
are not necessarily the most talented. And every-
body knows that could never be the case.

The Philosopher and the Horse

I cannot remember exactly where it happened.
It was somewhere in a square in Italy. I am pretty sure
it was Turin but, then again, it might just as easily

have been either Rome or Milan. I am also
unsure of the year. It must have been sometime in
the nineteenth century. A philosopher of note –

in fact, one of the most original thinkers of his
or, indeed, anyone else's time – broke down when he saw
a horse being whipped by its owner. The philosopher

threw himself around the horse's neck, allowing
his own flesh to come between the owner's whip and
the flesh of the horse. The philosopher, screaming,

was dragged away by his friends. I think the horse
died; if not directly due to the beating it had been given,
at least soon after. The owner of the horse gave

little thought to the event, it being, for a while,
a talking point at dinner parties. The philosopher,
on the other hand, never wrote another word.

Twins
for Desmond and Eddy

We got there just in time to see them
but still too late to be present at the birth.
One of them was lying in the farmer's

field drying, having been licked clean
by its mother's tongue. The other was
in the process of being cleaned,

and occasionally nudged, by the mother's
muzzle to encourage it to stand. As we watched,
it tried a few times, each one more

commendable than the last, but none
of them a complete success. By the time we left,
its wet head was still glistening

in the mid-May sun and its first step,
towards what would be an independence
of sorts, had not yet begun.

Speaking of Nim

The question is not, 'Can they reason?'
nor, 'Can they talk?' but, 'Can they suffer?'
                              – Jeremy Bentham

What the hell is that short for anyway?
What kind of name is that to give anyone,
especially a chimpanzee whose mother

was called Caroline? In any case, he was
taken from her when he was very young to be
raised as a human being so that we could

learn whether or not he could sign.
His second mother was a hippy who had
never looked after a primate before

and did not know how to sign. She had
had a fling with the professor whose project
it was. Unsurprisingly, this state of affairs

did not last long. Nim was then taken
to a more scientific establishment; his third
mother being an ambitious young student.

Nim took to her and his vocabulary grew.
He grew too and became too much of a hand-
ful. The professor finally pulled the plug

on the project saying, that although
the chimp could sign, he couldn't do so
grammatically. The project had,

fundamentally, been a failure. Ten years
on, Nim was in a private zoo when his second
mother decided to visit him. Ignoring

the owner's advice, she entered Nim's
cage. He roughed her up a bit; dragging her
around his enclosure by one of her ankles

like a rag doll. They said he could have
killed her if he had wanted to but he did not.
Five years after that, aged twenty-six,

Nim died of a heart attack. Although
he could sign, throughout his life, as if to
prove the professor right, Nim never

did produce a grammatical sentence;
nor, in spite of years of injustice, did he
ever sign a single angry word.

Nim Chimpsky (1973–2000) was a chimpanzee who was the subject of an
extended study of animal language acquisition at Columbia University.
Chimpsky was given his name as a pun on Noam Chomsky, the foremost
theorist of human language structure and generative grammar at the time.

A Fate Worse Than Death

Today, I signed a petition, online,
to save the bees from a fate worse than death,
although including it – the threat

of mass extinction. And yet, even that
had to be couched in terms of how it might affect
us humans. How, without the bees

to pollinate our crops, over a third
of the world's food supply would cease to exist.
Is it not enough for us to want

to try and save a fellow being
for its own sake? Or is it our fate to be interested
only in what concerns us? The fate

of megalomaniacs – to nurture
only that which supports our own existence;
our own idea of life on Earth.

Power Animals

What sort of animal is it I like
the most? Is it the sort I think I can
relate to, like a mother elephant,

hanging around the body of her dead
calf too long for it to be anything other than
a show of mourning? Or is it one I feel

I can't, like a predatory shark, forever
on the go, on the lookout for a whiff of blood
to follow so that it can slice a swimmer

in two? To tell the truth, it would have
to be something in the middle, like a company
of wolves. I like the fact that they live

in packs and look after their young.
I also admire the way they hunt down their
prey; living on flesh and blood. Perhaps,

there is just too much of the human
about them. I guess, in the end, I'll just have to
chose between the elephant and the shark.

Pros and Cons

Pigs are unable
to look up. At least
that is what a poem
told me once.

That means they will
never see the full moon
nor a shooting star as
it crosses the night sky.

Nor, however, can
they see the humane killer
as it glides towards them,
also from above.

Rats

Here, everything runs on time. And here,
everything is clean. So much so that a divorce
might be granted if either the husband,

or his wife, should make it to the platform
a few seconds late. Or a love affair might be ended
if the other man, or the other woman,

should forget to brush their teeth. And yet,
here, as everywhere else, there are rats. You can
see them watching, from the side

of the tracks. You can see them polishing
their teeth underneath the neon sign of the local pharmacy.
Or you can see them on a summer's night,

in the middle of a city, strolling, unashamedly,
through a park, with one eye on the eighteenth century
palace, and the other on the main chance.

Night and Day

What is the difference between
a butterfly and a moth? And don't just say when
we see them. Don't just tell me they are

as different as night and day.
One has more substance, more weight, more gravitas.
The other has more beauty, more lightness,

more joie de vivre. And what about
the similarities? Both of them love light. One, the sun
reflected by flowers; the other, by the surface

of the moon. And neither of them
has long to live. A week or so in which to find
a mate and breed. One of them comes

in a coat of many colours, the other
is usually black or brown. One of them, if cornered eats
your wardrobe; and neither makes a sound.

Spells

I have heard it said that there are
books containing spells to raise the dead
and others that can summon the Devil
himself. Just a few words, here and there,

to conjure up any creature of flesh
and blood would be enough for me. But
what if I could not control the being
that appeared? Even a common or garden

bat might be too much to handle.
Just imagine it flying out from the corner
of a page and landing in my hair.
Perhaps a single bite behind the ear would

be enough to give me rabies or,
at least, a course of painful injections,
just to be on the safe side; just
in case I started foaming at the mouth.

The city is not a jungle, it is a human zoo.

Desmond Morris

Part Five

A Temporary Perch

The Sky Tries

Suddenly, the sky has become more
important, as has each and every individual
member of the bird species. Clouds have

replaced waves and a pair of magpies
have had to stand in for a flock of seagulls.
A solitary crow is trying its best to caw

as loudly as the last skein of geese
that honked above our heads on the day
we turned our backs on the sea.

Rain Succeeds

It is a good day, as they say,
for ducks, or to remind a Scotsman
from where he has come. The rain is
pouring steadily, and the paths

through the East London Cemetery
are covered in yellows, browns and reds.
It does not bother me living so close to the dead.
It is something I have done for most

of my life. I have never been able
to bury them properly. They raise them-
selves from time to time inside my head. My heart,
however, has become somewhat harder.

Perhaps, the odd stray tear for some
of the more recent arrivals. The others,
though, are kept alive only by memory; by thoughts,
perhaps, but no longer by feelings.

The Florist

I like the florists across the road.
I like how industrious the people who work
there look; opening up first thing

in the morning; getting all the stock
out; wrapping, selling and delivering all day;
before locking up just before sunset.

I think it is a family business; a mother
and her daughter manning the shop; the father
in charge of the delivery van. They are

in a prime spot, only a few steps away
from the East London Cemetery. Till Death
Do Us Part means nothing to them.

Without death they would not be
able to make a living. The flowers, too,
look happy with the situation; such

a small time on the shelves and then,
a shortish carry, before fulfilling their ambition,
to be lovingly laid at the side of a grave.

The Lawn Inspector

If you watch a crow walking,
after a while it is hard to imagine
it in flight. Its stride is so well-

measured, so resolute, that
you think, for an instant, that earth
must be its true element.

This one is inspecting the lawn.
At times, it looks as if it is listening
to the grass growing, at others,

it gives the impression that
it might even be reading each blade.
To get a better look it removes

the odd fallen leaf. Suddenly, it
registers another life form and starts
to dig. After a few stabs, it extracts

an earthworm from the ground.
Once it has swallowed it, one cock of its
head is more than enough

to signify that it is time to leave.
In the flash of an eye, mine not its, it is
airborne and rapidly out of sight.

Lord of All

He is the lord of all he surveys, even
though it is not that much, less than an acre
of lawn and a handful of trees. Still,

he likes to keep his beady eye on things,
his feathery finger on the pulse. Even if just
a single sparrow stirs, he likes to know

about it. You can tell how much he hates
the magpies and the squirrels; their obvious lack
of responsibility. The foxes, he can relate

to; always on the look-out for something
to scavenge, some leftovers to take back home
to the den. The gulls, on the other hand,

confuse him. He cannot imagine what
they are doing in the middle of a city. They, who
if they had stayed put, could have had

the whole of the coastline to call their own.

The Philosophy of Facebook

It is the same flawed philosophy
behind Facebook; the one that says
if a tree in a forest is not seen

to have fallen, then no tree fell.
If you do not put up a post saying you have
written a poem, then the poem

does not exist. Taken to the extreme,
it means that unless you have shared something
with the rest of the world or, at least,

with your designated friends,
or friends of friends, then nothing actually
happened. Once again, the private life

is dead. For example, that fox I saw
last night in the garden is only now alive
because I have shared it with you.

The Black Mamba

I am convinced that
there has been some kind
of mistake, a misnaming,

as I watch a pale green snake
slither across the floor of its cage.
I am just about to inform one

of the keepers when I read
that the reason it is called the Black
Mamba is because of the colour

of the inside of its mouth.
That little morsel keeps my one
firmly shut.

Dragons

There are two of them, but one
would have been more than enough.
Their presence is excessive;

their very existence, a threat
to my own. I do not need to be told
that one of them was in a fight

scene in the latest Bond film.
The very idea of Daniel Craig defeating
one of these creatures strikes

me as ridiculous. I choose one
to look at and try to concentrate. It looks
at me too, each of us a statue,

separated by nothing but a pane
of glass. I am sure that, if it wanted to,
the beast could shatter it. A single

bite would be enough to kill me.
Even if I did escape, the bacteria in its
saliva would, eventually, do

the trick. It would then track me
down and devour me. I decide to leave
and visit some of the other cages,

but I have to go back for a final look.
The chosen one has not moved a muscle,
nor even blinked a single eye. I am

afraid I find its stoicism repulsive.

A Starling at Camden Lock

Everybody here is a wannabe; hoping
against hope to be the next big thing; everybody –

including a metallic starling perched
on top of the rusty guttering of a designer
shop in Camden Lock. And the starling

has got it just right. She has come out,
mid-morning, after the briefest of downpours,

with the sun now shining and her plumage
sparkling. All she really wants, just like the rest
of us, is to be seen; to be recorded

for posterity; to end up in a natural history
documentary, or on the cover of a magazine.

A Cormorant in Regent's Canal

Midway, between the house-boats
and the canal-side apartments, a cormorant
is in the act of disappearing

and returning. The passers-by call it
fishing, and they are right to do so. The bird,
no more than a stone's throw

away from us, is unmistakable. As it
surfaces, a man standing behind us, with much
paternal authority in his voice, tells

his children, "Look, boys, there's a grebe!"
It reminds me of a poem by Lucia Perillo in which
another father mistakes a coyote for a wolf.

She attempts to correct him, but
the man sticks to his guns and will not budge.
I let the present misnaming go.

It is late April, the sun is out, the wind
is warm, and the cormorant itself does not seem
to mind. It dives once more to resurface

with a sliver of silver. Thankfully,
the father on the towpath does not try
to name the species of the fish.

A Robin Into Africa

A robin redbreast sits upon the branch
of a tree in the middle of a city – the perfect
visual image of Christmas. And yet,

this one is set at the edge of Into Africa
in London Zoo. This robin's neighbours are
neither foxes nor sparrows, but hunting

dogs and gorillas. What a tale it will have
to tell its grandchildren about all the exotic animals
it has seen and all the places it has never

been. This place is just one step away
from a virtual reality. Turn the next corner
and you leave the Savannah and enter

the Australian bush. The robin remains
unfazed by it all. At any moment, it can switch
it off and see its tree, and the branch

it is sitting on, for what they really are -
a temporary perch in the short life-span of a native
species; a bird who has no knowledge

of the five continents that are on display,
nor of the Christmas which, to us, it represents,
little more than a fortnight away.

A Heron at Penguin Beach

Amongst all the Rockhoppers,
the Black-footeds, and the Humboldts,
there lurks an impostor … the Grey-Haired.
Although not the most animated

member of the troop, he is still
the most impressive. Whilst the others
bob about in the Antarctic waters, waiting
to be thrown their lunch, he stands

imperious at the edge. He has
already fed elsewhere on living flesh.
This is where he comes to rest. At any moment,
he could unfurl himself and make a great

escape. I wonder if the others
know this. So not in their element,
it will soon be time for them to walk their
walk for the paying visitors. With

a ruffle of his feathers, the heron
settles down to ignore the show. After
another forty winks or so, he will rouse him-
self, extend his wings, and go.

Acknowledgements

Some of these poems previously appeared in the journals *The Antigonish Review, Gutter, The Malahat Review, Northwords Now, Other Poetry, Poetry Ireland, Poetry Scotland, Southlight, The Best of British Poetry 2011* and *The Interpreter's House*.

'The Black Mamba' and 'Dragons' will appear in the 2014 Spring issue of *Message in a Bottle*.

'A Sign' will appear in *Ink Sweat and Tears* in August 2013.

Cultured Llama Publishing

hungry for poetry
thirsty for fiction

Cultured Llama was born in a converted stable. This creature of humble birth drank greedily from the creative source of the poets, writers, artists and musicians that visited, and soon the llama fulfilled the destiny of its given name.

Cultured Llama is a publishing house, a multi-arts events promoter and a fundraiser for charity. It aspires to quality from the first creative thought through to the finished product.

www.culturedllama.co.uk

Also published by Cultured Llama

A Radiance
by Bethany W. Pope

Paperback; 70pp; 203x127mm;
978-0-9568921-3-3; June 2012
Cultured Llama

Family stories and extraordinary images glow throughout this compelling debut collection from an award-winning author, like the disc of uranium buried in her grandfather's backyard. *A Radiance* 'gives glimpses into a world both contemporary and deeply attuned to history – the embattled history of a family, but also of the American South where the author grew up.'

'A stunning debut collection ... these poems invite us to reinvent loss as a new kind of dwelling, where the infinitesimal becomes as luminous as ever.'

Menna Elfyn

'*A Radiance* weaves the voices of four generations into a rich story of family betrayal and survival, shame and grace, the visceral and sublime. A sense of offbeat wonder at everyday miracles of survival and love both fires these poems and haunts them – in a good way.'

Tiffany S. Atkinson

'An exhilarating and exceptional new voice in poetry.'

Matthew Francis

Also published by Cultured Llama

strange fruits
by Maria C. McCarthy

Paperback; 72pp; 203x127mm;
978-0-9568921-0-2; July 2011
Cultured Llama (in association with
WordAid.org.uk)

Maria is a poet of remarkable skill, whose work offers surprising glimpses into our 21st-century lives – the 'strange fruits' of our civilisation or lack of it. Shot through with meditations on the past and her heritage as 'an Irish girl, an English woman', *strange fruits* includes poems reflecting on her urban life in a Medway town and as a rural resident in Swale.

Maria writes, and occasionally teaches creative writing, in a shed at the end of her garden.

All profits from the sale of *strange fruits* go to Macmillan Cancer Support, Registered Charity Number 261017.

'Maria McCarthy writes of the poetry process: "There is a quickening early in the day" ('Raising Poems'). A quickening is certainly apparent in these humane poems, which are both natural and skilful, and combine the earthiness and mysteriousness of life. I read *strange fruits* with pleasure, surprise and a sense of recognition.'

Moniza Alvi

Canterbury Tales on a Cockcrow Morning
by Maggie Harris

Paperback; 136pp; 203x127mm;
978-0-9568921-6-4; September 2012
Cultured Llama

Maggie Harris brings warmth and humour to her *Canterbury Tales on a Cockcrow Morning* and tops them with a twist of calypso.

Here are pilgrims old and new: Eliot living in 'This Mother Country' for half a century; Samantha learning that country life is not like in the magazines.

There are stories of regret, longing and wanting to belong; a sense of place and displacement resonates throughout.

> 'Finely tuned to dialogue and shifting registers of speech, Maggie Harris' fast-moving prose is as prismatic as the multi-layered world she evokes. Her Canterbury Tales, sharply observed, are rich with migrant collisions and collusions.'

> John Agard

The Strangest Thankyou
by Richard Thomas

Paperback; 98pp; 203x127mm;
978-0-9568921-5-7; October 2012
Cultured Llama

Richard Thomas's debut poetry collection embraces the magical and the mundane, the exotic and the everyday, the surreal rooted in reality.

Grand poetic themes of love, death and great lives are cut with surprising twists and playful use of language, shape, form and imagery.

The poet seeks 'an array of wonder' in "Dig" and spreads his 'riches' throughout *The Strangest Thankyou*.

> 'He has long been one to watch, and with this strong, diverse collection Richard Thomas is now one to read. And re-read.'
>
> Matt Harvey

Also published by Cultured Llama

Unauthorised Person
by Philip Kane

Paperback; 74pp; 203x127mm;
978-0-9568921-4-0; November 2012
Cultured Llama

Philip Kane describes *Unauthorised Person* as a 'concept album' of individual poems, sequences, and visuals, threaded together by the central motif of the River Medway.

This collection draws together poems written and images collected over 27 years, exploring the psychogeography of the people and urban landscapes of the Medway Towns, where 'chatham high street is paradise enough' ("johnnie writes a quatrain").

> 'This collection shows a poet whose work has grown in stature to become strong, honest and mature. Yet another voice has emerged from the Medway region that I'm sure will be heard beyond our borders. The pieces here vary in tone, often lyrical, sometimes prosaic but all show a deep rooted humanity and a political (with a small p) sensibility.'
>
> Bill Lewis

Unexplored Territory
edited by Maria C. McCarthy

Paperback; 112pp; 203x127mm;
978-0-9568921-7-1; November 2012
Cultured Llama

Unexplored Territory is the first anthology from
Cultured Llama – poetry and fiction that take a
slantwise look at worlds, both real and imagined.

> 'A dynamic range of new work by both established and
> emerging writers, this anthology offers numerous delights.
>
> The themes and preoccupations are wide-ranging. Rooted
> in close observation, the poems and short fiction concern the
> 'unexplored territory' of person and place.
>
> A must for anyone who likes good writing.'

Nancy Gaffield
author of *Tokaido Road*

Contributors:

Jenny Cross	Philip Kane	Hilda Sheehan
Maggie Drury	Luigi Marchini	Fiona Sinclair
June English	Maria C. McCarthy	Jane Stemp
Maggie Harris	Rosemary McLeish	Richard Thomas
Mark Holihan	Gillian Moyes	Vicky Wilson
Sarah Jenkin	Bethany W. Pope	

The Night My Sister
Went to Hollywood
by Hilda Sheehan

Paperback; 82pp; 203x127mm;
978-0-9568921-8-8; March 2013
Cultured Llama

In *The Night My Sister Went To Hollywood* Hilda
Sheehan offers poems on love, exhaustion, classic movies, supermarket
shopping and seals in the bathtub. Her poems 'bristle with the stuff of
life'. Her language is 'vigorous and seductively surreal'. 'What kind of
a mother writes poems / anyway, and why?' she asks. A mother of five,
Hilda Sheehan is that kind of mother. Read this debut poetry collection
now: 'time is running out … Asda will shut soon'.

I was constantly impressed by a sense of voice, and a wonderful
voice, clear and absolutely achieved. Throughout ... domestic
imagery makes of the kitchen and the household tasks a
contemporary epic. The deceptively trivial detail of our daily
lives works just as in Dickens, a great collector of trivia, and
the pre-Raphaelites, revealing a powerful gift for metaphor. As
Coleridge said, metaphor is an important gift of the true poet,
and Hilda Sheehan has that gift in abundance.

William Bedford
author of *Collecting Bottle Tops: Selected Poetry 1960-2008*

It's one thing to have a vivid imagination. It's another to be adept
at language. It's quite another to be gifted with the language
to release and express that imagination. Hilda Sheehan has all
three. She has the ability to see the pathos – as well as the joie
de vivre – in the human comedy, and to convey it in a vigorous
and sometimes seductively surreal language. We are enabled to
see what we may not have been able or prepared to see, or even
thought of seeing: this is what poetry is all about.

Robert Vas Dias
author of *Still-Life and Other Poems of Art and Artifice*

Also published by Cultured Llama

Notes from a
Bright Field
by Rose Cook

Paperback; 104pp; 203x127mm;
978-0-9568921-9-5; July 2013
Cultured Llama

Rose Cook's *Notes From a Bright Field* is 'a single quiet
path, in and out', capturing the transitory beauties of the everyday:
a mother's ashes imagined as 'Lux flakes'; the 'fruit-gummed glass'
of a cathedral. Where the poems' themes are of nature, loss and the
spiritual, these are grounded in concrete imagery like 'the clack-clack
of the shell and the bones'.

> In their transparency and deceptive simplicity Rose Cook's
> poems reveal pure and hidden depths in nature, memory and
> loss, celebrating and questioning the fragility of everyday inter-
> actions. These are indeed poems for people 'who juggle [their]
> lives', insisting in their gratitude that we 'be still sometimes'.
> To read *Notes From a Bright Field* is to be renewed in body, mind
> and spirit.
>
> Anthony Wilson
> author of *Riddance*

> Rose Cook's poems are often poignant, reflecting the many vari-
> ables of ordinary lives, but always with a lightness of touch, an
> acceptance of what it is to be human. A collection fluid and sin-
> cere, the poems are wide ranging, sometimes painterly, some-
> times with a wonderful down-to-earth diction and a singular
> inwardness that delights.
>
> Denise McSheehy
> author of *Salt*

Lightning Source UK Ltd.
Milton Keynes UK
UKOW04f1924110913

217036UK00001B/2/P